AN ISLAND FROM THE AIR
THE SECOND FLIGHT

Hinton and Manby

ISLAND BOOKS

NEWPORT, ISLE OF WIGHT

For Eileen, my pilot on the ground.

First published in Great Britain in 1995 by Island Books

Island Books is an imprint of Ravenswood Publications Ltd, London

Copyright © 1995 by Brian Hinton and Brian Manby

Environmental notes copyright © 1995 by Davyd Morgan-Moore

ISBN 1 898198 05 5

British Library Cataloguing-in-Publishing Data
A catalogue record for this book is available from the British Library

Designed, Printed and bound by Crossprint Design & Print
Newport, Isle of Wight

Sole distributor
HBS, Newport, Isle of Wight

Front cover: Medina River at Cowes
Rear cover: Yarmouth Town and Havenstreet Railway Station

35 Norris Castle

"With a fair and easterly wind, we successfully sailed along the woody and beautiful coast of Binstead, Wootton and Whippingham."

Norris Castle is set on this coastline, dominating the seashore which appears bottom left and facing Southampton Water. This is a landscape of palaces, a rich terrain indeed with which to conclude our flight. Further along the shore is Old Castle Point, all that remains of the Tudor defenses. Over the brow of the hill is a modern housing estate, built on the ground where John Nash's East Cowes Castle once proudly stood. Top right is New Barn, in the middle the green acres of a golf course, and top left the park of Osborne House.

Built by James Wyatt in 1799, Norris Castle is a kind of mock Carisbrooke, a historical fake. Even the adjoining farmhouse has crenellations and turrets, like a child's fort. The sea wall is constructed from Swanage stone. It was here that the twelve year old Princess Victoria first stayed, in 1831, and where she first began her love affair with the Isle of Wight, consummated at Osborne.

In Rosamond Lehmann's strange book "The Swan in the Evening: Fragments of an Inner Life", she describes places where time seems to stop, or rather where she actually steps outside time, for brief but lifetime-enhancing moments, into eternity. Many poets and artists have reported the same phenomenon, and devoted a lifetime to trying to recapture it.

For Lehmann, the Isle of Wight seems particularly rich in this quality, and she tries to puzzle out why this should be. "Perhaps the regal auras of Queen Victoria and Charles I still lend the Island air a higher vibratory frequency; perhaps the murmuring shade of Alfred Lord Tennyson still brushes the birds, and the tides; perhaps the vestiges of pre-history scattered over and beneath its turf and chalk and sandstone account for the magical atmosphere of certain woods, downs, valleys, chines, undercliffs and standing stones ..."

Whatever the reason, the Island traps and encodes time. As befits the Dr Who exhibition at the Needles Pleasure Park - itself kitted out like a Pharoah's palace - Wight is a kind of Tardis, travelling through space. The trappings and costumes might change. The essentials do not.

As Henry Wyndham found, while taking his grand tour here during the closing years of the 18th Century, Island roads even then had their frustrations, the need to rely on ferries - as now - imposed extra difficulties on those used to the comforts of the mainland.

"Horses, and carriages of all kinds, may be hired at Newport, by those who may not choose to bring their own over the water. The party cannot be too early in engaging them, as there is a most extraordinary demand for them during the summer months."

Looking at these photographs, captured forever in summer sunshine and redolent of warmth and green shade, one can still see why.

Index to photographs

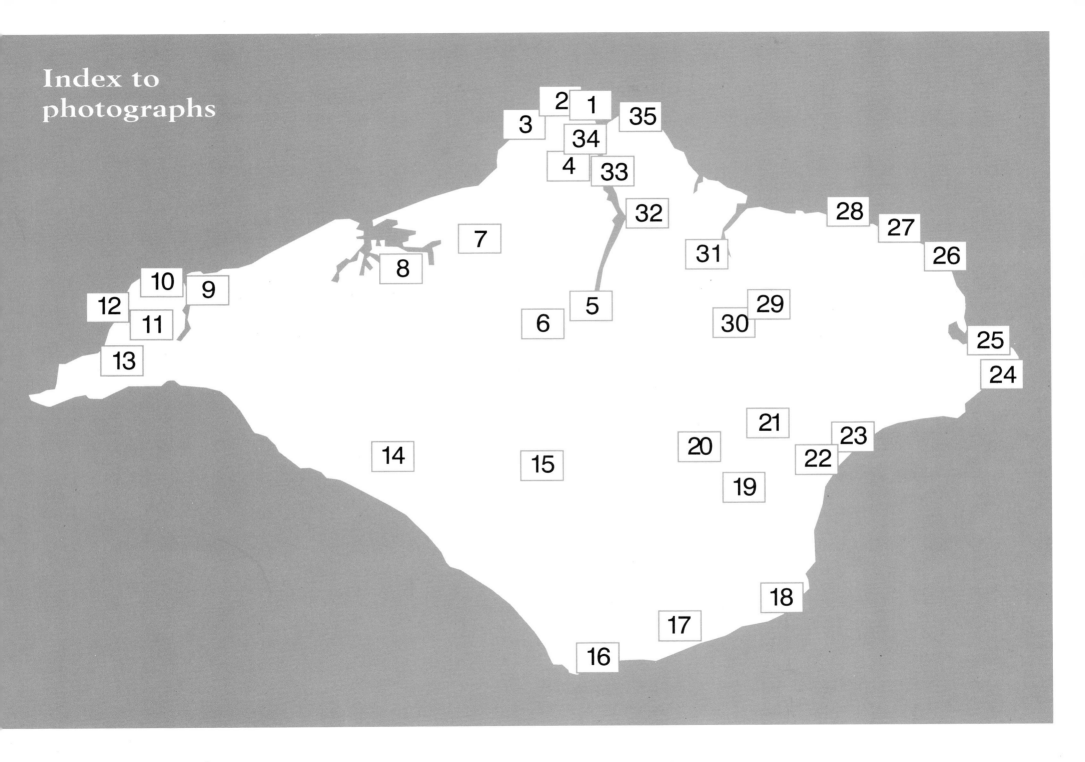

1 West Cowes

"The town and harbour of Cowes opened their busy and lively scenes to our passage."

It is Cowes week, and this Rip Van Winkle of Island towns has woken from its annual slumber, which this photograph freezes again into a moment of time caught forever. Past and present are revealed through the camera's lens as welded together, though this photograph itself is already a relic, as much part of history as the dinosaurs.

In just the same way, Henry Wyndham's chatty but accurate "A Picture of the Isle of Wight", first published in 1794 - from which I also quoted extensively in the first volume - often seems bang up to date. The essentials have barely changed at all.

This is a landscape of jumbled particularities, of history as a living process. Centre left is Medina House, where Uffa Fox lived, and Thomas Arnold - pioneering headmaster of Rugby - was born. Arnold's father was Collector of Customs at East Cowes; his son a famous poet. Time makes strange comparisons. At the bottom of the picture is Spencer Thetis Wharf, where square rigging is constructed for Hollywood, using age-old techniques. The shed-like building on the corner is Clare Lallow. It was here that, in a previous incarnation, J Samuel White - now just a name on an adjacent wall - constructed the first flying boat.

For the time being, everything is static; yachts and power boats moored in Cowes Yacht Haven, cars parked like multi-coloured dinky toys in crowded streets, people reduced to tiny dots around the blue and white striped marquees. It is all like the start of Alfred Noyes' strange novel "No Other Man", where the hero comes ashore on the Isle of Wight to find everybody dead.

There are signs of life, though, if one looks closely enough. A solitary car is waiting to turn right out of Birmingham Road. The RNLI lifeboat chugs out to sea in middle channel, while a few small boats move to and fro in front of the hydrofoil terminal, and Cowes Parade.

2 West Cowes

"We could not but regret the waste of so much fine water, which would be invaluable in many parts of the north side of the island, and particularly at Cowes, where even bad water is so scarce, that we not only bought it for every family use, but also for washing the wheels of our carriages, and we even paid a weekly acknowledgment for the permission of watering our horses, in what would be considered on the opposite coast of Hampshire as a common horse pond."

The waters of the Medina here encircle and define West Cowes. They service alike the exclusive pontoon of the Royal Yacht Squadron, pleasure boats moored on the Parade to take trippers to see the Royal Yacht, and the industrial boatbuilding yards (just out of picture top left) of Clare Lallow and Groves & Guttridge.

Our viewpoint has turned almost 180 degrees, with the 1930s splendour of Osborne Court - like a multi-tiered wedding cake - dominating Cowes Parade. The open building site beside it is now The Gloster. Here are the anchorages of those to whom the sea is an open road, the Royal London Yacht Squadron, the Royal Corinthian and - grandest of all - the Royal Yacht Squadron with its red striped awning bottom right.

As befits naval warfare past, the small cannon just visible on the sea wall in front is real, one of those that directs the races out in the Solent beyond. Top right is St Mary's Church, its tower redesigned by John Nash, and the beginnings of Northwood Park. Above, a red brick maze of modern housing is interrupted by a large stone building (out of picture) which seems to have dropped in unannounced from Classical Greece, or the English Age of Elegance.

The gentle curve of the Parade, ending in the stern block of HM Customs, is echoed by two elegant semicircles - Bath on Solent. That to the right provides sheltered seating and a grandstand view of the Solent. A plaque on the wall commemorates the embarkation here, in 1633, of the Ark and the Dove, off to establish the state of Maryland, under charter from Charles I.

A one way street - its "No Entry" markings clearly warning us even from this height - leads past high class restaurants and bookshops, galleries specialising in maritime art and purveyors of high class sweets to the portals of Cowes Business Centre - where Brian Manby plies his trade, when not airborne.

Our own journey will instead take the scenic route west - as Wyndham did by sea one memorable day in 1794. From the giant's viewpoint of our Cessna, we will

3 Gurnard

"Having passed by Egypt, a house so called on the sea shore, about half a mile from Cowes, we rode through a country inclosed with hedges, but barren of trees, to Gurnard's Bridge: here was anciently a seaport, but at present, a common wherry is rarely to be seen in its contracted channel."

Egypt Point is just off shot here to the left; the woods above on Egypt Hill conceal a military emplacement. In the centre is Solent Middle School, and a large sports field. Beyond is Cowes High School and Northwood Park, part of its circular wall still visible to the right, fronting Baring Road. Top right is East Cowes, its breakwater stretching out across the Medina's mouth, and Old Castle Point on its northern extremity.

At the bottom of the picture is the calm, waveless blue of Gurnard Bay facing a line of bathing huts - it is not as innocent as it looks; bottom right, the rocks lead to Gurnard ledge - and Princes Esplanade, which sweeps royally back to Cowes, opened by the Prince of Wales in 1926. The large building which dominates the green is the Woodvale Inn, home to some ferocious pub quiz contests.

Hidden in the trees - at one point the Island was so thickly forested that "a squirrel might have run on the tops of the trees from Gurnard to Carisbrooke" - are some eccentric summer residences, fairy tail constructions in painted and carved wood. The road running off bottom right is Rew Street, which we will meet again, in a most unlikely place.

"It has been supposed, from the two words, which in the French and English languages are synonymous, that Rue Street, near Gurnard's Bay, was part of a Roman road, which commenced at Gurnard's Bridge, and that it passed in a direct line from thence, through the forest of Parkhurst, to Carisbrooke. As no vestiges of such a road, either in Rue Street or in the forest now remain, I am inclined to think that such an idea was the visionary system of some antiquarian, more zealous to support a discovery of his own, than to be contented with the common history of the Island."

4 Northwood

"The roads are excellent on each side of the Newport River. The parish church of Cowes is at Northwood, to which that on the hill of Cowes is only a chapel of ease, though it is of much larger dimensions than its mother church. A long ascent leads from Cowes towards Northwood, and the inclosed country continues to the Forest Gate, from whence the naked heath reaches for nearly two miles."

As the relative status of the two churches indicate - Northwood Church is just out of shot middle right here, adjoining the Agricultural show ground - Cowes is an outgrowth of Northwood, a cuckoo which has come to dominate the nest.

West and East Cowes are beautifully delineated here, pin sharp in the sunlight, as a ferry heads off north to Southampton. Northwood is now a place of industry and commerce. Middle left is the large Siemens Plessey works, photographed before the radar tower was built; further to the left are Readers and Vikoma.

The great wood of Northwood is now reduced to the three remaining areas - like green propellers - surrounding Medham House, with Somerton Copse to the left, Calving Close Copse to the right, and Waterclose Copse in in front. Behind, edging up to the cycleway from Newport, are Bottom Copse and Shamblers Copse. Ward's Copse is bottom left.

The rest of the land is given over to agriculture - the field systems edged with ancient hedgerows - industry and modern housing. Oxford Street - home of the surrealist poet David Gascoyne - snakes down to meet Wyatts Lane at the bottom of the picture, with Northwood Primary School on the left. For those seeking fine ales, The Travellers Joy is just off to the left, as Pallance Road leads towards Porchfield.

The main road from Newport to Cowes winds diagonally upwards, taking a sharp bend into West Cowes. On the right, Northwood cemetery adjoins a small reservoir. Even after compulsory water metering - for which Islanders paid the installation costs - lost to history are the disgraceful scenes that Wyndham witnessed, the Cowes water riots!

"Such has been the scarcity of water in the neighbourhood of Cowes, that the poor part of the inhabitants has been known to arrest and empty the water carts, on their passage to the town, in the same violent and outrageous manner as if a famine should compel them to plunder either meat or bread, for the immediate satisfaction of their craving necessity."

5 Newport

"After passing the Medina, behind the Mills of Newport, we soon entered upon the large and open fields of the farms of Pan and West Standen. Here is no appearance of the neighbourouring seas, and its district is as well calculated for the diversion of coursing or partridge shooting as the best sporting counties of the kingdom."

The Pan estate - open fields no more - begins bottom right, but the locals now have less bloodthirsty diversions to help them pass the time.

Top right is Newport Quay, flanked by the Quay Arts Centre, the squash club and the Riverside Centre. Middle left are the shed like buildings of a leading DIY firm, adjoining a prominent Island book shop. Just out of shot is Brannon House, HQ of the Isle of Wight County Press - whose pages list a cornucopia of jumble sales, barn dances, illustrated talks in echoing church halls - and the Apollo Theatre.

Like a giant scalextric set, the Medina Way - the Island's largest stretch of dual carriageway - snakes down to the Coppins Bridge interchange, picked out by sunshine from the adjoining cloud shadow. To its right is Little London and the Riverway Industrial Estate, doubling back to Dodnor, where this book was given birth, at Crossprint.

Like most market towns, Newport is a cat's cradle of history; even its streets stay true to the medieval town plan. Top left is the old Grammar School where Charles I signed the Treaty of Newport in 1648. On the High Street, Georgian shop fronts give way to the brutal, modernist contours of County Hall. Time can heal as well as hurt. At the very edge of the picture is "Read's Posting House", once terminus for the mail coach from Freshwater, its arrival notified by a blast on a post horn, later a garage. Suitably renovated, it opened in 1995 as the offices for the IOW Rural Community Council, a phoenix from the ashes.

Middle left, on the very edge of the picture, is the old Town Hall, part designed by John Nash, which will soon reopen as a museum dedicated to tracking the Island's past. The unbiased eye of the camera is perhaps a more trustworthy guide as to how past and present combine to odd and sometimes comic, sometimes tragic effect.

6 Carisbrooke Castle

"We returned from Standen, and pursued a bridle-track to Carisbrooke Castle, the outward fortifications of which, by trespassing through some inclosures, we surrounded and surveyed with much pleasure.

The castle has been enlarged and extended at different periods, but perhaps no part is older than the Norman Conquest, as the high keep, which appears to be the most ancient structure, was not in use before that time. The outward fortifications are said to have been added by Queen Elizabeth. The walls and bastions are perfect in many places, which may be well surveyed by a walk or ride, round the circumference of the castle.

The well is the greatest curiosity within the walls of the castle; it is 200 feet in depth, and produces, in the driest seasons, water of the purest quality. It is common for strangers to drop a pin into this well, the depth and echoing vault of which reverberates a sound, when the pin touches the water, that is really astonishing. It is also common to drop a lighted sheet of brown paper into the well, when the reaction of the air beneath, upon that which is rarified by the flame of the paper, keeps it somewhat buoyant, and makes it descend in so slow and spiral a direction, that the whole cavity becomes discernable, till the fire is extinguished in the water below."

Little has changed in two centuries. Carisbrooke Castle stands proudly on its parcel of land, like a toy fort. To its right, county council vans and lorries are parked, like dinky toys, in the Island Group 90 depot - semi privatised in the 1979 Revolution - neatly sandwiched between the ancient walled Priory and Mountjoy Cemetery.

Top right a road proceeds in a regal curve to Carisbrooke High School; beyond lies the green gloom of Parkhurst Forest, edged by the white bulk of the waste recyling plant, like a breaking wave.

The spire of Carisbrooke Church dominates centre shot. Just in front, Lukely Brook broadens into the Southern Water pond behind the 8 Bells pub car park. To its left is a tiny roundabout - scene of many a near fatal collision. From this ancient crossroads, Gunville Road leads north past MFI and Argus. Their high tech sheds catching the sunlight. Clatterford Road leads off middle left to Bowcombe and Shorwell, and Calbourne Road snakes off due west past farms and open fields towards Swainston and Freshwater. At the top of the picture is the Solent, with the mouth of Newtown river gaping in the far distance.

"Our road conducted us under the outworks of Carisbrooke Castle, which we left on our right hand. We then entered into a broad and pleasant vale, intermixed with woods, arable fields and pastures. Sir John Barrington has a handsome seat at Swainston, situated in the midst of a wide and sylvan domain."

7 Porchfield

"Between Rue Street and Thorness is a small farm, called Whippence, which from the circumstance of the scarcity of trees in this part of the island, deserves some notice, from its being finely shaded by a considerable range of tall elms, that so disposed as to form a rich boundary to a wide and semicircular lawn, which gradually descends from the farm-house towards the shore."

We are looking due south, back towards Carisbrooke, towards which New Road points like a giant finger. In the middle distance, the patchwork quilt of fields and ancient hedgerows is interrupted by the straight line of Forest Road. This leads on the far left of the picture, between Westwood Dairy and a petrol station, to the extreme edge of Parkhurst Forest. To the right, the road bends sharply past Trumor Feed and straightens out towards Shalfleet. At the crossroads, Whitehouse Road becomes Betty Haunt Lane, its slight incline in the middle a bridge over the now non-existent railway line, and leading up to the Calbourne road.

To the left and just visible beneath the foothills of Bowcombe Down is the Blacksmith's Arms,whose barmaid rests so uneasy. One dark night, friends of mine were driving up the narrow lane when, for no reason, all the car's lights failed to work for a few moments, plunging them into utter darkness. They have never taken this short cut since!

Whippence Farm - and the road back to Gurnard - are off left, past the village centre, with the Sportsman's Rest and Post Office clearly visible. Bottom left, the green clump of trees marks the edge of the sinisterly named - and shaped - Coffin Copse. To compound this sense of hidden danger, bottom right, past Lambsleaze Farm, is an army camp, and the start of the firing ranges at Clamerkin. These are not mere games, as the War Memorial at the crossroads amply testifies.

Just off the bottom of the picture is Elmsworth Farm and a footpath to the muddy shoreline. On the bottom edge of the picture, centre, are boarding kennels, behind which sheep graze peacefully in the fields. Rodge Brook meanders through the village.

It is as if time has stopped in this photograph, to a soundtrack of Elgar, and Rupert Brooke sadly asking if there is honey still for tea. That is, until one sees the strange white marks cut into the field to the left of the crossroads, like an ancient maze. Intrigued, I approached them to find instead a large bungalow already constructed on them since this picture was taken.

8 Newtown

"Newtown sends two Members to Parliament; the Town-Hall stands by itself, in which are elected the representatives; the rest of the village, as it now has no church consists of a few straggling cottages, though there are visible remains of ancient streets, and of a much greater population.

No spot, perhaps, upon the terrestial globe shews more evident proofs of the gradual succession of the sea, than this Island. The numerous salterns, and the many narrow valleys were indisputably ancient creeks;those which still remain have visibly left long tracks of deserted land above them. Within the time of history, some of these are known to have been even ports or harbours."

The Town Hall leans there still, just to the right of the old town of Newtown, picked out now in hedgerows and green fields, not stone and brick. To its left is Noah's Ark, a 13th century Inn. To its left, a verdant lane continues the one still inhabited road, Gold Street, into the deeper green of Walter's Copse.

It is only from the air that one can reconstruct the archaeology of the place, and step back through history to rediscover the original town, before the French left it waste and looted. Still visible are some of the old field systems, 22 yards long by 220 yards wide, tilled in medieval times. To the left, another green lane leads up from the old Coastguard cottages to join the current road.

Newtown nestles between the two blue arms of Newtown river, centre right, and Clamerkin Lake, top left. In the far distance are the army barracks of Jersey Camp and - like three parallel cricket pitches - the butts for rifle practice. Spent shells abound here, both military and aquatic. Since Roman times, Newtown has been a catchment area for oysters and clams, now grown in tanks hidden away in the depths of the forest. Indeed, Newtown itself is like an oyster opened for the camera, its promontory of land rich in history and silt.

Its original name was Francheville, or Free Town, and it was the premier port of the Island. Sailors and longshoremen worked busily at their trades here. The empty shoreline was once a hive of industry. Reasons for decline differ. One is the gradual silting up of the north coast, matching the gradual erosion of the Back of the Wight. The Isle of Wight is gradually moving to rejoin Hampshire! Another is a succession of raids by the Danes - under Sweyne, who gave his name to Swainston - and the French, culminating in the invasion of 1377, when frightened villages took refuge in the sturdy tower of Shalfleet Church. Most bizarre of all is a variant of the Pied Piper legend, in which the rats were led down Gold Street to drown in the Solent.

For whatever reason, we now look down on mudflats, and a footbridge which crosses bottom left to the Nature Reserve. Even the Church of the Holy Spirit, dead centre of this picture, was built as late as 1837. This is a place of ghosts. Newtown is back to Nature, with a vengeance.

9 Yarmouth

"At Yarmouth Sir Robert Holmes, the then Governor, had built a large house, and in which he entertained King Charles II. This house is now the inn.

If there should be any traces of an old road in any part of the forest, it might probably be that which was expressly made by Sir Robert Holmes in 1671, for the accomodation of King Charles II who, after landing at Gurnard's Bay, pursued his journey to Yarmouth through the forest of Parkhurst."

We too have followed the route of Charles II's royal progress - with a brief detour to the place of his father's less happy Island holiday. Charles would find Yarmouth itself barely changed, but its surroundings radically altered. As at Newtown, silt has encrusted the river estuary; here the process has been assisted by man. On reclaimed land - the borders of 17th Century Yarmouth can be traced by the city wall circling back from the ferry terminal - now sit a car park, a boat park, and rich grassland, even a row of trees.

The Pier was built in 1876 as a deep water terminal for the London and South West Railway Company. It turns sharp right at the end, and the Round House on the jetty is a necessary refuge in bad weather for the keen sea-fishermen who prove its most loyal inhabitants. Many of them helped preserve the pier by private subscription, and the names of these proud benefactors are carved into the planks, like tombstones.

Until 1951, paddle steamers would land here, bringing the likes of Julia Cameron home or to visit. Mrs Cameron gave some of her photographic portraits as a free gift to be placed in the ferry terminal, now Gossips Cafe. The young WH Auden once walked down the pier in an extraordinary hat, saying how boring he found Nature. Local children found him a subject of great amusement.

In 1938, the current Pier Head was built, with roll-on, roll-off facilities for modern car ferries. One ferry has recently embarked; another is approaching from Lymington River, top left, the masts of moored yachts like a forest of tooth picks. The pier head, and its approach lanes can be clearly seen, to the left of Yarmouth Castle, whose Governor's dwellings are now the George Hotel, recently bought by a member of Dire Straits.

The breakwater which created Yarmouth harbour was built by 1847; it snakes to almost join the pier head like a black adder, running in parallel to the new road bridge. Mill Copse stretches out bottom right - its twin tentacles almost touching the footpath which follows the line of the old railway track from Yarmouth station, now a youth club and clearly visible here - Saltern Wood is bottom left. Yarmouth nestles compact, dominated by the spire of St James Church, opposite the 18th Century Town Hall, with fine Georgian houses facing the sea. The Royal Solent Yacht Club is to the right of the pier, an exclusive enclave in this most exclusive of Island towns.

10 Yarmouth Bridge

Here our viewpoint shifts by 180 degrees, and pans in to focus on the new automatic swing bridge. Two curved white lines mark the section which swings at right angles to allow tall masted yachts access to the river Yar. It is local rumour that shortly after this million pound project was completed, urgent repairs had to be made when pigeon droppings gummed up the works.

Top left is Yarmouth Mill, once the home of the historian AJP Taylor, who understood the ebb and flow of the past, and who I remember sitting in front of the ancient New Buildings of Magdalen College, Oxford, an old man beached by time. In front and on the edge of the shot is the local garage and the back of Yarmouth Primary School, scene of many a charity fete.

Bottom left, in Yarmouth harbour, is the RNLI lifeboat "The Joy and John Wade", safely at anchor for the present, but a reminder that yachting is not all moored gin palaces and deck shoes. Any harbour provides safe - and temporary - respite from the open sea, excitement but also danger. Behind is the white bulk of the Yarmouth Saiing Club, and to the left a lorry approaches the ferry check in.

To the right is Hales Boat Yard. Its premises span the centuries, half modern and functional, half the long "L" shape of the 19th.C "Sand House" - pointing to the small quay - used originally to store sand dug from Alum Bay and shipped off to glassworks on the mainland. Alum Bay now boasts both coloured sands - saleable in their own right - and a glassworks which produces local craftwork, locally designed.

The green marker which guards Hales' entrance from the main road is the Black Rock buoy, out of its natural element, and oddly reminiscent of the Black Knight rocket whose test launch site was at Alum Bay. On the other side of the road are salt marshes, a haven for bird life, and top right is Saltern Wood Quay, access to which is further down the road, past a circular house in the woods and Puffin Fisheries and Yarmouth Pottery. This is a working landscape, where boats are scraped free of the sea's residue.

Top right, the Western Yar leads out of shot to Freshwater; it is navigable right up to the Causeway, beyond which it rises in the marshes just north of Freshwater Bay. We are now entering an island - give or take a few yards of soil - within an Island.

"Off Yarmouth, the hamlet of Norton, on the opposite bank of the Yar, showed some signs of richness, while its scattered cottages among the frequent groves were not unpleasant to our inquisitive eyes."

11 Golden Hill

"Many pleasant spots are to be found in this sequestered parish, and the little hamlet of Norton exhibits some rural cottages that have lately been erected, with more expense, indeed, than taste."

Taste is not timeless. Norton Green is off left, a delightful village with a historical preservation order on it, but lacking a pub, chapel or village shop. One house escapes the aspic. The artist Mignon Jones lives in an 18th.C home with perfect classical proportions, studded with her strictly modern paintings and sculptures. Just in shot here, though, is Norton Green Holiday Park, with its caravans, its mobile homes and its swimming pool.

Half hidden is the Norton Green Industrial Park - some park! - a small industrial complex which leads to Golden Hill Works and other remnants of the light engineering factories which once made Britain great and are now as much endangered species as the golden eagle or the otter.

History and commerce meet at Golden Hill Fort, the hexagonal building centre top. Completed in 1867 to defend the Solent, it became a school for gunnery - AA Milne was based here before he left for the trenches, to put his new-found skills to use - and is now a home for craft workshops, and a military museum. More recently, it has hosted the strobe lights and booming bass lines of electronically manipulated "rave" music, much to the consternation of local residents. I wandered past late at night, and thought war had broken out, with the shadows of chemically enhanced revellers dancing on the battlements. I hope that they did not meet the fort's resident ghost; it might have literally pushed them over the edge!

Surrounding the Fort is Golden Hill Country Park, a green lung at the heart of the wild west, where Yarmouth blends into Colwell, into Totland, into Freshwater. To its right and top left modern Freshwater intrudes, ever spreading.

The block of largely modern housing at the bottom of the picture is, or was, Solent Hill. The blocked windows of the building with twin brick outcrops, like sentry boxes, promises older mysteries. It is the local Masonic Hall, its entrance porch emblazoned with strange insignia, like Egyptian heiroglyphs, looming large over the surrounding countryside, and even larger in the minds of local conspiracy theorists. As an honourary "lady" at my father's lodge's annual dinner dances, I fear they would be sadly disappointed at the reality, local businessmen doing good work for charity.

Speaking of which, the imposing building bottom left is Green Meadows, a Methodist home for the elderly. The main road from Yarmouth to Freshwater curves across the photo, with Heathfield Road leading off past the summer home of Tennyson's friend Granville Bradley. Bottom centre, Monks Lane leads down to Brambles Holiday Centre and Fort Albert, and the sea, to which this picture resolutely turns its back.

12 Fort Albert

"The land begins now to ascend to some height; the whole soil is a stiff clay, and declines from the hills to the shore, while the sunken separations, and the wide chasms of the long slope, both ancient nad modern, were very apparent to our vessel."

Fort Albert was built in 1856 as a military emplacement. Later it became a torpedo station; now it houses luxury flats and its own jetty.

Cliff End Battery guards the land above, its shape now picked out in barrack like holiday homes. The past endures, even if in disguise. There are even local rumours, half believed, of a series of underground tunnels which link all of West Wight's forts in subterranean darkness, like a warren of man-sized rabbit burrows,.

Off to the left is the coastal path to Fort Victoria, now hosting an aquarium and planetarium, as well as thrilling views across the closest sea passage between Island and mainland on to Hurst Castle. At twilight, to the smells of summer barbecues, yachts flit across in front of the country park like Arab dhows.

The cliff-edge here is just as unstable as in Wyndham's time. Thanks to "blue slipper" clay, the sense of impermanence which even granite and chalk contain is speeded up here. Everything is in flux, uncertain, prone to collapse. Just like modern life, in fact.

The boundaries between sea and land are ever changing. I have often watched cliff falls in progress along this coast, a spill of soil which the sea then carries away over the next months until it is as if these tons of loose debris had never been. Not for nothing is this called Cliff End. Everything balances insecure: the still clearly visible gun emplacements - like concrete doughnuts - holiday chalets, cars parked on the cliff edge. In another century or so, the marks of man here will probably be in the sea, like footsteps fading on the sand.

Of course, this all brings a sense of adventure to the dull, everyday world. To the right is Brambles Holiday Centre, gloriously impermanent. It all adds to the zest of the holiday.

13 Colwell, Freshwater Bay

"The highest elevation of this long hill is called Afton Down. The prospect from it reaches almost around the whole Island, and far beyond the opposite parts of Hampshire, farther indeed, than the best eye can command. The cliffs of the Isle of Purbeck are distinctly visible from it, but an unvapoured atmosphere is necessary to mark those of the Isle of Portland, with the same precision."

The same unvapoured atmosphere here facilitates our aerial view from Colwell Bay - just down the coast from Fort Albert - back over Freshwater to Afton and Tennyson Downs, with the coast to Blackgang stretching out in the far distance.

One can date this picture as having been taken after Autumn 1992 by the absence in Freshwater Bay - if my failing eyesight is not playing tricks on me - of The Arch Rock. For so long a local landmark, it quickly succumbed to the waves one fierce October day. As soon as word spread, visitors poured in to see it in absentia, as if mourning their own past. Postcards of the Arch Rock still in place were soon fetching a premium; there was even a commemorative booklet and exhibition.

To start at the beginning, at the bottom of this shot is Colwell Bay, with jet skiers throwing their patterns as spray disturbing the deep blue of the Solent. A solitary yacht passes more sedately, heading for Warden Ledge on the right of the photo, its sharp rocks hiding under water but not from us.

Brambles Chine to the left has coloured sands almost to rival Alum Bay. Bathing huts and groynes both signify a mecca for keen swimmers, as do the tiny dots of holidaymakers on the sandy beach. Behind are all the other necessities of summer, cafes and souvenir shops, guest houses and holiday chalets, a large car park and public loos.

Colwell Chine Road leads up from the sea, past the green acres of Colwell Common, to where modern housing zigzags through remaining fields to the Bay. There one can clearly pick out the white magnificence of the Holiday Fellowship hotel and Fort Redoubt, now tearooms. Farringford skulks off to the right, half hidden among sheltering trees. To the left, Afton Road snakes down to the Bay, with All Saints Church just out of shot up Hooke Hill, and Afton Down clearly showing the golf course, and the start of the Tennyson Trail. In the far distance the Military Road leads off top left towards Brighstone.

Chalk arches may come and go, carved from the cliff by the action of waves which eventually carry them off as well, but in over two hundred years the real essentials of this landscape remain the same.

"The coast of Mottistone, Brixton, Shorwell and Chale exhibited its long, waving and comparatively low cliffs to our view."

14 Brighstone

"The village of Brixton, or as it is pronounced by the natives, Briseton, is clean and populous: its church has a short stone spire upon a low tower, which form is also followed in the architecture of those at Shorwell and Mottistone. From Brook Down we admired the four parishes of Shorwell, Brixton, Mottistone and Brook, the lands of which are sheltered by the high downs from the north, and which, from that circumstance, and their uninterrupted exposition to the meridian sun, receive a more genial warmth, than the British latitudes are naturally entitled to.

Exclusive of this advantage, these parishes contain the best corn lands in the Island. The fields are large and well inclosed with quickset fences, but scarcely a tree is to be seen in the hedges, that can afford shade to the fly-teased cattle during the summer heats, or shelter from the impetuous fury of the winter's storm."

The church is just off shot to the middle right. Clearly visible though are the mysterious circles of the sewage works, hidden from the road into Brighstone by thick woodland, which here conceals Grange Chine. Just off camera at the bottom is the Military Road, leading to Barney's Roadhouse with its nightclub, a Friday night mating ground for local youth. To the top right is the Worsley trail to Shorwell.

The bungalows and mellow farmhouses of Brighstone stretch along the valley. Moortown Lane winds past upmarket B&B's and a gnome's house to a disused chalk pit and Brighstone Down. On the other side of the thickly wooded chalk ridge - the Island's spine - Lynch Lane leads to Calbourne. Beyond lie Shalfleet and Newtown Bay. To the left, and out of shot, Westover Down leads to a line of neolithic barrows, looking down almost cosily onto the Long Stone at Mottistone, our mini - and singular - Stonehenge. Ancient man inhabited the downs, not the valleys.

Cosiness is certainly the order of the day in Brighstone, with its tea rooms and picturesque cottages - much used in TV sit-coms - its thatched post office and tiny branch library. Everything is of manageable size; the Junior School - middle left - winding lanes (imbued with typical English eccentricity) which deny the village a natural centre, even the herd of prize Jersey cows at Shate Farm.

Sheltered under its ridge-top, Brighstone looks like Paradise on earth. Wyndham went back to classical antiquity for his comparisons.

"Here is little to entertain the eye of the casual passenger, but extensive fields and a boundless expanse of ocean. The industrious husbandman, however, thinks this want of beauty well compensated by a perpetual supply of the finest water, and by the great abundance of corn ricks, which surrounding and adorning their farm-houses, are so accurately formed into an oval shape, and so closely thatched with their own strong and unthrashed straw, that they seem to have been modelled from the sepulchral vases of Greece, or of ancient Rome."

15 Shorwell

"Two or three rich farms lie in this narrow vale, at the end of which is the parish street of Shorwell, and adjoining to it stands North Court. This is a large ancient house, and was erected in the early part of the reign of James I. The east front still maintains its original purity, and is built with a smooth and durable stone, that is now rarely to be met with in the insular quarries. The square projecting windows, the casements pendent on their stone mullions; the seated porch and gable-end roof, give this side of the building a venerable and not unpleasing appearance.

The house is surrounded by hills, naked, but not uncultivated, nor unfruitful: however, a large grove of trees, probably coeval with the building, affords shelter and shade to the garden walks: a partial view of the English channel opens from one of the higher seats, which I should scarcely have noticed, if we had not enjoyed the fortunate moment of viewing from it the uncommon prospect of twenty ships of the line, with every sail spread, and moving before us, with an easy gale of wind, within the distance of five miles from the shore."

North Court, carefully and lovingly restored by the Harrison family, who bought it semi-derelict, is clearly visible centre shot, like a grey egg in a circular nest of trees. Above and to its right is a massive chalk pit, a scar on this ancient landscape whose depredations are only fully visible from the air.

Shorwell shute is hidden in overhanging foliage, with its 18th.C wooden bridge spanning the chasm of the road far beneath. Long gone is a hunting lodge made of sheep's bones - the heady scent of wild garlic remains - and a temple to the sun; the weird byways of history are retained in the name of Mt. Ararat, into which the chalk pit burrows.

Perhaps a second ark will be launched from these green acres, to save us from the great flood we are promised with global warming, and the melting of the ice caps. This land has been under water before; otherwise how would the chalk downs have arisen from the deposit of countless generations of sea dwellers.

Back to earth, the Newport road winds away towards the back of the picture, through Bowcombe, up to Carisbrooke village just visible top right. Rising to the left is Cheverton Down, and the road back to Brighstone.

Shorwell is a strange mixture of modern estates and thatched cottages. St Peter's Church and the Crown Inn dominate the village centre, to the bottom left is the moat and gable end of Wolverton manor, built in the shape of an "E" to commemorate the first Queen Elizabeth, and haunted by a minstrel, whose ghostly fiddle tunes can be heard late at night. Swinburne's "one loose thin, tremulous vein" of water rises here, to join with the Buddle and flow to the sea. Park Lane heads towards us, and Atherfield. Bottom right, Sandy Lane leads on past Kingston and on to Chale, towards Niton and the Undercliff.

16 Niton and Puckaster Cove

"Moving from Niton, we soon descended by an oblique road on the side of the rocks, to what is called the Undercliff. If the mind of any person can remain tranquil on the first view of this wonderful country, or if he can gaze with indifference on the sublime scene above and below him, I do not envy the cool phlegm of his constitution, but I should advise him to confine his future airings to the level and dusty roads that surround our metropolis."

Castlehaven Lane winds down - neither level nor dusty - to a caravan park. Reeth Bay is bottom left; to the right is Puckaster Cove. Niton straddles up the hill - the Buddle Inn is centre left, with a car park and look out point to St Catherine's Lighthouse. Steps lead down to Castlehaven Lane. The main road bends back in a one-way system up Sandrock Road - named after the freshwater spring whose waters proved so fashionable in the early 19th century - past ancient stone walls, back to an ornate house like a small French chateau and the petrol station.

Barrack Shute winds uphill, with the Methodist Church on its left, to the main village. A left turn leads past the White Lion pub, purveyor of live jazz in the winter, then doubles back past the Church, where Edward Edwards is buried, architect of the free library service, currently in free fall.

The land to the left of this picture is also in (slow) motion, leading to Blackgang and what was once the lower road, remnants of which now cling to the edge of a high granite cliff. Above Reeth Bay the magnificent Victoria hotel plunged to the shore while its royal patron was still on the throne.

The source of the Eastern Yar - whose progress we will follow - rises behind the upper village; south of Ladyacre Farm and Head Down. The road to Whitwell heads up top right, past Kingates Farm. In the centre, the road leads up towards Godshill and past the site of the original 1968 Pop Festival at Bleak Down; Marc Bolan's Tyrannosaurus Rex played within sight of the dinosaur coast! Cows now graze peacefully in the quiet fields.

Bottom right are the "fairy palaces" of the start of Undercliff, which inspired Wyndham's longest and most involved sentence, and idea.

"When I reflect upon the various houses, that have been erected upon whimsical and capricious plans, some founded upon the inconvenient designs of a Gothic College, others resembling a church, with its tower and chancel, it has been a matter of surprise to me that no eccentric genius has ever conceived the idea of imitating the designs and elevation of the stern of a ship of war: which might be erected at much less expense than many of the modern and fashionable "cottages".
No spot could be more properly appropriated for the foundation of such an edifice, than several of the projecting rocks, on the coasts of this undercliff."

17 Undercliff

"This undercliff properly begins at a small house called Knowles, which is placed on the low southernmost point of the Island, under the hill of St Catherine's. The distance from Knowles to Bonchurch, which is the eastern termination of the Undercliff, is nearly six miles, but they are such miles as are not, for their singularity, perhaps to be parallelled in the whole world.

Bold cliffs, low lands, or declining shores and the usual boundaries of the ocean, but on this extravagant coast, a wall-like rectilinear precipice of lofty rock extends itself for some miles in length.

In this interval of rock and water, colossal fragments of stone, torn or sunk by some great convulsion of nature, are scattered below, in the most irregular confusion. These solid masses are of such ponderous magnitude that they form high eminences of the most capricious shapes, while their intermediate spaces become deep valleys, in which houses are built, and even ashes and elms are seen to flourish."

This is no holiday beach. The Mediterranean blue of the sea - on this, the Island's Riviera - breaks at the bottom of chalk cliffs, on savage boulders. Middle right is the Rare Breeds Park, with Lisle Combe just on the edge of the picture, once home of the poet Alfred Noyes, who tended a famous garden here. Orchards Bay - which he took as the title of perhaps his finest prose work, reprinted as the "Incompleat Gardener" - is just off to the right, subject to a long dispute between local citizens and the owner.

Parallel to the sea is the road from Niton to Ventnor. Just visible through the trees is the new St Lawrence Church, designed by Gilbert Scott and with Pre-Raphaelite stained glass saved from the Royal National Hospital and a line of houses ornate and huge as Indian palaces. Just above the wooden look-out tower of the largest is St Lawrence under Wath, the 12th.C old church, with its tiny graveyard. The railway line is now a line of houses a near precipice leads up to St Lawrence Shute - emerging here into green fields towards Stenbury Down. Week Farm is top right, the cliff-top road runs from Whitwell to Upper Ventnor.

Out of shot to the left is Old Park Road, the Tropical Bird Park and Isle of Wight Glass, whose swirling, mystic patterns evoke the strangeness - and weird clarity of light - of this landscape. Off to the right is Rew Lane, continued down from Gurnard, the ancient trackway of the sun which bisects the Island north to south ...

"Some faint idea of this wonderful country may perhaps be conceived from the above description, which from the towering hills above, appears to the eye like a level plain; but which, when seen from the sea, rises like a series of gigantic steps. The houses of St Lawrence are interspersed between the majestic ruins of nature, and its little diminutive church is erected upon one of its fragments, but which indeed contain a surface sufficient for the foundation of a cathedral."

18 Monks Bay, Bonchurch

"We are now arrived at the east extremity of this singular Undercliff, which is closed at Bonchurch with an impassable promontory. We were therefore obliged to ascend by a steep and zigzag road, through the rugged crags of a declivity, to a high spot.

A safe, though precipitious, coach road has been long established from the Downs to Steephill. Having left my reader on the summit of Bonchurch Hill, I shall now accompany him, through the large and fertile fields of its brow (from whence we may look down on a picturesque farm, called Luccomb, and on the opening of its little chine) to a hanging wood, through which we descended to the verdant pastures of the neat and pleasant parish of Shanklin."

At the top of the precipice Bonchurch Down and St Boniface Down merge in a weird amalgam of ancient tumuli and more up to date mysteries. Radar and radio masts aim for the sky. Here too is a nuclear bunker, tunnelled deep into the rock. Also concealed from our view, and just off camera, is the railway tunnel driven through this sheltering promontory to Ventnor station, now an industrial estate.

Bonchurch village shelters underneath the down. Leeson Road, at the top, runs east past Nansen Hill, and off to Shanklin. Bottom left are East Dene and Winterbourne, the temporary haunts of Swinburne and Dickens who met here when one was already a great novelist, the other a "golden haired" young boy. Both swam in Monks Bay, but neither could have imagined the temporary island out to sea - now no more - from which was constructed the new coastal defenses.

Even they cannot forever protect the strange, shifting world of the Landslip, the wooded area off to the right, from the local "blue slipper" clay. A small spill can be seen oozing onto the beach, as it edges round to Dunnose. It now seems like an augury. In February 1995, $1\frac{1}{2}$ million tonnes of debris crashed down at roughly this point, in the most serious case of subsidence seen here since 1818. The County Press quoted a local fisherman, still in shock. "It was a horrendous sight - the earth, trees and walking trails were rolling over like a constant waterfall". Not for nothing did the poet John Keats write during a visit here in 1817 his famous sonnet on the sea:

"It keeps eternal whisperings around
 Desolate shores . . ."

Tucked safely - for the moment - behind the Downs is Wroxall. Out of shot to the right is Luccombe. The spelling has changed since Wyndham's time, the Chine has propelled itself further into the English Channel.

19 Apse Heath

"We turned from Princelet Shoot into a cart road, through arable fields, which led us to Apse Farm, and from thence, at the foot of the mountainous cliff of the parish, to Shanklin."

In folklore a crossroads is a place of great danger, of encounters with the spirit world and hanged men; it was where the American bluesman Robert Johnson met the devil. The one here seems prosaic when driving round its mini roundabout - like a white tiddlywink - on the main road from Newport to Lake. Viewed from the air, it is seen in context, an ancient meeting place of two "cart roads", cut into a rich and settled landscape.

Ventnor road leads up from Wroxall. Just out of shot is Little Princelet Cross, where the road divides off towards Newchurch, and a small lane leads back to Apse Manor Farm and America Wood. Apse Heath itself is flat prairie - the fields are large and still arable - interrupted by strips of modern houses, dominated by the Spar shop at the crossroads, with its car park cut into a field opposite. What looks like a 2nd World War air-raid shelter is on the right, its roof overgrown and fast returning to Nature.

To the left, backing up to the houses is a small lake covered with reed beds. Beyond the Newport road, leading on the right to Lake past the Methodist Church, is Alveston Road, a small track on the right leads to Bigbury Farm, and the lorry yard of George Jenkins Transport.

Giant pylons march across the fields, carrying the modern voodoo of electricity. The road continues up to a new housing estate, on the edge of Winford, and past Borthwood Copse. When I last drove past, some local wag - or trickster - had turned the signpost round, especially to confuse visiting motorists. Folklore is alive and well, at the end of the second Millennium AD.

20 Newchurch

"An uncultivated heath connects this wood with the populous street of Newchurch, the church of which is large and stands upon an eminence, that commands most parts of the circumjacent country."

Just by Borthwood Copse, off top right here, the road divides at a sharp bend. Alverstone Road continues to the north. Skinner's Hill winds down steeply to a valley, past Puck Farm, then rises as Palmer's Lane. It can be seen clearly here, snaking down into the lush valley past Devonia Nurseries on the middle right.

Newchurch crests the hill, the white boarded steeple of the (by now) ancient church facing us centre left, just before the high street plunges down a steep hill towards Knighton, and its ghostly manor house, of which only the gates now remain. The Pointer Inn is next to the church, with Butts farm behind, and Alverstone Garden Village fronted by Youngwoods Copse in the distance, at the top of the picture.

The strange, maze like markings centre right - "tailt turns" following the contours of the land - belong to Cockerell Field, with redundant nursery buildings at its entrance. They are the result of circular ploughing, but quite why I am at a loss to explain. Perhaps we have a Glastonbury-type mystery unfolding before our eyes, sighted only from the air. After all it is on such high, sacred hills - Godshill is a case in point - that ley lines collide, and where churches were built on sites already long steeped in psychic energy.

More prosaically, yellow vans front the garage, and just off shot to the right - and the road back to Winford - is Wackland Lane, home of Osel Enterprises.

21 Alverstone

"A rough and steep descent brought us to the neat little hamlet of Alverton, and soon after we arrived at a poor and beggarly cottage, placed on the point of a high insulated knoll, called the Queen's Bower, which, by a popular tradition, is supposed to have been a spot from whence our ancient queens enjoyed the views of the chase around it.
This elevated site attracts the eye from every road in the vale.
Bordwood is still an extensive wood, and covers half of the circular hill of the Queen's Bower, with its thick shade."

At first glance, at the centre of this picture is a second "extensive wood", matching Borthwood Copse, top right. We have shifted our viewpoint 90 degrees from the previous photo, and now look back at the Newport road at the top of the picture, with Apse Heath on the right, from whence we came.

But all is not as it seems. What we are actually overseeing is Alverstone Garden Village, one of the most exclusive housing areas on the Island, and here half buried in vegetation. It was built between the wars, like the Collins estates across the Solent in Southampton, as an attempt at elegant living, creating a modern village for rich suburbanites. Despite some modern infilling, there remains a sense of space and order. A maze of cul de sacs wind up and down steep hills, the whole lost in green shade and cultivated anonymity. Whether it works or not as a community is not for us to judge, looking down from our own commanding height.

Newchurch is invisible on the right. In shot is Youngmans Copse. To the far left is the road to Alverstone which leads just out of shot over a stone bridge, crossing the Eastern Yar, which then passes over a footpath where once steam trains puffed their leisurely way from Newport to Sandown. The line - or its absence - can be seen sinking through the bottom of the woods.

The lake - or flood - at bottom left does not appear on my map, so I leave it as a mystery to explore some other day. Alverstone Road leads up diagonally, with Burnt House Lane on the left, between the strange knoll of Queen's Bower - its surmounting cottages neither poor nor beggarly to modern eyes - and Borthwood Copse. There it branches right down Skinner's Hill or upwards into Winford, where a straight track doubles back to the Newport road. Top left, Lake begins its urban sprawl.

Sandown airport lies in the fields between, the birthplace of this flight, but a place to pass over for now as we make for one of the modern wonders of the Wight, a Lake where no man can swim!

22 Lake

"Though not large, the neatness of every cottage, the park-like lawns, the acclivities around them, enriched with coppices, and with respectable ashes and oaks mark Shanklin as a spot where we might naturally expect some noble mansion. But alas, none is to be found, nor is there any tradition that human art has, at any time, contributed to render this scenery so pleasing to the spectator."

Lake is the mid point of the long strip of modern "civilisation" which unites Shanklin and Sandown, in one endless round of holiday fun. The noble mansion of our times, manor house and cathedral combined, is the out of town superstore, and here centre stage is Safeways, with its attendant petrol station like a stable block to the left.

In front - like tenants' cottages - is Lake Industrial Way, on the left, and a redundant factory, Lake Temperature Works, on the right. Rumour has it that its sheds are soon to be flattened for a modern housing estate: Whitecross Lane leads out of shot to Lower and Upper Hyde. To complete this portrait of late 20th.C power points, Lake Middle School lies to the left as the road enters the village proper.

It is not without significance to my thesis - history repeating itself endlessly, with bizarre variations - that Safeway now opens for part of Sunday. Its parishioners prey in the aisles, queueing for absolution at the checkouts.

Some have escaped the encroaching tide of brick and concrete. At bottom left, someone has pitched a pink tent among the trees. Behind Safeway, on the delightfully named "Merrie Gardens", a white marquee fronts two lines of either smaller tents or caravans, laid out with military precision. Scotchells Brook leads under the main road, to the flatlands beyond.

Everywhere - from this height - are toy cars, miniature trees, model buildings, sunning themselves. But, like a science fiction fantasy by Wyndham's later namesake - whose heroes escaped the Triffids by fleeing to the Isle of Wight - there is not a single human being to be seen. Perhaps they are all swimming in the non-existent Lake!

23 Sandown

"The aspect opens to the ocean, and takes in the whole of Sandown Bay; a grand and noble object formed by the chalky cliffs of Culver on the east, and on the west by the craggy rocks of the mountainous point of Dunnose, six miles distant from each other."

Two hundred years ago, this coastline was almost bare of human habitation. Fishermen based in the small hamlet of Lake - somewhere in the middle of this current sprawl - began a small bathing enterprise, using spa waters which came down the cliff in natural springs. This is the result.

Sandown Bay still opens its aspect to the ocean, or at least the English Channel. At the top the cliffs bend round at Horse Ledge, towards Luccombe and Bonchurch: the strange radio masts we saw earlier reappear on the far horizon. Sandown Pier pierces the Bay; its neighbour at Shanklin was demolished in 1992. Just visible in the near distance are Rylstone Gardens and Keats Green on Shanklin clifftop, the lift down from the Promenade, and the mouth of the Chine, with the Smugglers Inn ready to provide refreshment. The old village is tucked behind the urban chaos. Sibden Hill rises top right.

Nearer to camera is Sandown. Once it was called Sandham, and in 1801 boasted only three buildings, the Fort - now a zoo - Barracks, now the South Wight Leisure Centre, and the ornate dwelling of John Wilkes, now lost to the sea.

This century has brought guest houses and hotels in jumbled profusion, and redefined terms from the past. Here are villas, catering for tourists. Here are estates. College Close Industrial Estate is seen bottom left, growing like Topsy, encroaching on land reclaimed from the waves. And here are parks. A caravan park and car park lead the eye delicately to crazy golf links and a bowling green, with the edge of the boating lake just visible bottom left.

The holiday coast leads off the picture towards the picturesque village of Yaverland, barely touched by the centuries, and Bembridge Down, edged by the slopes of Culver Cliff, white as a vanilla ice.

A boat approaches from the left, leaving white water in its wake. Unawares, it retraces in reverse Wyndham's great adventure, his circumnavigation of the Island.

"We now, in the seaman's phrase, doubled the great point of Dunnose, and were passing at some little distance from the chine of Shanklin and the fort of Sandown, at the Culver Cliff, when the sun closed his setting rays on us."

24 Bembridge

"We now ascended Bimbridge Down, on the top of which are some large corn-fields, that divide the Down into two nearly equal parts. We rode through these fields to the end of the farther part, where its whole outline is terminated by the chalky precipices of the Culver Cliffs.

We returned from this Down to Longland Farm, from whence the road conducted us, along the shady lanes, near the Harbour at Brading, and close to a windmill, to the farm of Foreland."

Brading no longer has a harbour; flat - and often waterlogged - fields now front it. The sea has retreated down the Yar valley, with some human assistance, leaving old houses to stare as if bemused at this drained landscape.

Foreland still forms the eastern extremity of Wight - as its name suggests - a muddy and flat counterpart to the Needles in the west. It is here top right. Slightly down and to the right, a bulge in the coast marks the position of the HM Coastguard station, in yellow brick, and the Crab and Lobster Inn, whose name gives an idea of the main harvest hereabouts. The coastal path winds back towards us and Whitecliff Bay.

To the left, the Lifeboat Station at Lane End juts out into the sea, like a Wild West wagon on a stick. It guards the notorious Bembridge Ledge, the darker patches in the enveloping blue, which presage shipwreck and violent death. Far away indeed from Bembridge's current reputation as a weekend home for yachtsmen, and the super rich.

Where once were fields, Howgate Road, parallel to the sea, and Steyne Road strike eastwards like giant tyre tracks, edged with modern housing developments. The private track to the left of Howgate Road is Forelands Farm Lane, which Wyndham might well have walked, is flanked by private mansions, and leads the intrepid motorist over potholes to Fisherman's Walk at Lanes End. Warner's Bembridge Village holiday camp lies beyond, fronting the coast.

We come back along Lane End Road, some of whose palaces boast high walls and electronic locks - Parkhurst prison in reverse - keeping the world at bay. Forelands Road leads left into the village centre, past the one time landed estates of the gentry. These flat acres now farm herds of tidy bungalows, the rich haunt of retired headteachers and upmarket bookdealers. Steyne Road leads back towards us past Bembridge Primary School and a recreation ground to the crossroads at Steyne cross, just out of shot bottom left.

Here a road leads further left, to Bembridge windmill, still in existence if tethered, and under the tenure of the National Trust. Faintly echoing the sea, swimming pools glint in the sun.

25 Bembridge Harbour

"We had sufficient twilight to enable us to distinguish the low lands of the peninsula of Bimbridge, the mouth of Brading harbour, and the sylvan shore of St Helens."

Our previous viewpoint has turned round by 90 degrees. We are now viewing the Island from the east, with the rising sun. Our first port of call is Warner's Bembridge Holiday Village, oddly reminiscent of Portmeirion as depicted in Patrick McGoohan's TV fantasy "The Prisoner" with its red brick mansion, its ornate chalets, its white portico. If it lacks a life size chess set - as yet - it already boasts a bowling green, walled with white, on which priest-like figures play patience yards from the beach and the sharp undersea rocks of Bembridge Ledge.

To accentuate the sinister, out to sea here and out of view - but somehow exerting their looming presence - are the "Palmerstone Follies", giant sized stone thimbles which guard the approach to Portsmouth. The wooden bridge to the Lifeboat Station leads out of shot on the right, like a launch pad.

The village centre is to the back of this "peninsula of Bimbridge", with the tower of Holy Trinity Church clearly visible, as a marker point. In a bold experiment, the local council abolished unilaterally all parking restrictions; the expected chaos failed to materialise, and the scheme is now regretted only by redundant traffic wardens.

Behind the church, and to the left, the shore road winds down past the burnt out shell of the Rowbarge - a pub built like a boat - and onto Bembridge Harbour. Here too a fine Victorian hotel was senselessly demolished - its drinking fountain still remains - awaiting the long mooted development, the scandal concerning which is still in recent memory. Past the Tollgate cafe and the white boards of the exclusive Bembridge Sailing Club - again straight out of "The Prisoner" - the road can be seen edging the harbour and its colony of houseboats, to cross the Eastern Yar bridge - recently reconstructed, though no yachts dare venture up this narrow creek - into St Helens.

In the far distance is Ryde, the coastline back to East Cowes, and Portsmouth just visible on the horizon. Across Bembridge harbour, The Duver - all that is left of a church and its graveyard swept out to sea - catches the sunlight, like a white monolith. Beyond on the coast is Church Butts and Haven Nodes Point Camp, and just in shot to the far right Priory Bay, its overlooking mansion now a luxury hotel.

"Priory House stands at the head of a very spacious lawn, that gently declines from the house to a high ridge, the steep bank of which is covered with wood down to the high water's edge. Views open to the greatest advantage to Spithead and Portsmouth, to St Helen's Road or to the Sussex coast, where they are, at length, lost in the boundless horizon of the east."

26 Nettlestone and Seaview

"At Nettlestone, about a hundred yards from the high road, but not visible from it, stands an elegant box of Mr Henry Oglander, who has, not improperly given it the name of Fairy Hill. it is a "ferme ornee", the fields of which are disposed in the happiest manner, and are all dressed with the neatness of a garden.

The lane, near the gate of Fairy Hill, leads to a place called Seagrove. A gentleman a few years since had intended to build a large house on this delicious spot, but as he lived only to see the stables completed, these are now fited up as a dwelling house, with tenements, and solely inhabited by poor inhabitants."

Seagrove Bay fronts this symphony in blue and green, dotted with - in turn - yachts and expensive modern housing. To the right, a jet skier turns back past Horsestone Point to Priory Bay; the road coming in from the right leads from St Helens to Ryde; it flanks a camp of tents and red roofs which provide a splash of violent colour in this eminently tasteful and wealthy neighbourhood. Wyndham's "tenements" and "poor inhabitants" have no place here any more.

Seaview colonises the outcrop of land at Nettlestone Point. Here an elegant late-Victorian iron pier led out 900 feet to sea, destroyed utterly by a violent storm in 1951. The Halland Hotel, given world fame when Bob Dylan sat on the sea wall outside grinning for the world's press, has been pulled down, its sea defenses half shattered already.
Bloodiest of all was the attempted French invasion of 1545, commemorated in a small monument by the Bay.

For all that, Seaview is - or at least appears - a calm repository of history, in its very names - Rope Walk, Old Fort Inn - and in the settled peace of the sailing club; Lloyds Bank nestles in a restored Georgian cottage. Other cottages which edge down to the sea are rich with English eccentricity, boat-like in their weatherboards and balconies, life-belts as ornaments.

There is something other-worldly about Seaview. It was here that I paid "Boy George", whose elegance oddly matched that of Seaview Hotel, in used fivers after the 1990 pop festival. It was also here that I underwent hypnotherapy after a car smash, settling into a calmer world. It all seemed appropriate somehow.

Up the hill, past allotments, Fairy Hill survives from Wyndham's time, middle left, still looking down over Seaview. Here, by Gibb Well and Nettlestone Hill, the Primary School and Nettlestone Green guard the road to Ryde. It leads off to the left, past a row of half-timbered cottages on the bend, whose names proudly echo the high ground of private education: Harrow, Eton, Rugby, Cambridge, Oxford, Radley, Winchester and Marlborough.

The coastline, meanwhile, edges past a toll road on to Puckpool and Appley.

27 Appley

"As it was not the time of high water, we drove along the shore to a house of Dr Walker, called Apley, which is charmingly placed on the high and woody margin of the sea bank, and from whence ascended, through two or three beautiful meadows, to the common road that leads from Ryde to St Helens."

Appley House has been long demolished, but its grounds remain, disguised as the housing estate, park and pitch and putt golf course at the bottom here. The crenellated folly of Appley Tower, built later by the Paymaster General, still mounts the sea wall. It presents itself regally, looming up toward the camera like a sky rocket, and casting a rounded shadow.

The "high and woody margin" of the sea bank remains, and the mud flats have been cunningly converted to the golden harvest of Ryde East Sands. Holidaymakers disport themselves, like ants. Towards the top of the picture is Ryde Pier with its railway line and ferry terminal. Ryde House appears top left, with Ryde West Sands leading on past Pelhamfield and onto Quarr.

The coastal path bellies out in the middle here, past a boating lake and outdoor swimming pool. To the left is St Cecilia's Abbey, above is the green lung of Simeon's Recreation Ground, and down to the left St John's Park. Wyndham records the original house, "of an elegant architecture" standing "on a lofty eminence, and in the centre of a large, sloping lawn, bounded by trees on every side".

Elegance is the order of the day hereabouts. The "beautiful meadows" noticed by Wyndham have long gone, built over by 19th Century villas, and Ryde - the Island Brighton - retains this elegance, often in spite of its local politicians. It was originally a hilltop village separated by fields from the humble fishing port on the coast. In 1780, one of the packways linking the two was laid out as Union Street, presaging the construction of a regency town. It was during this time of transition that Wyndham made his visit.

"Ryde has two tolerable inns, with chaises and whiskies. Many decent lodgings are also to be hired in the place, and decked vessels, or boats, may be engaged on its quay, at ten minutes notice. While we made a pause at this village, we were recommended to a wooden bench about a hundred yards below the inn.

We had hitherto been amused, in this morning's ride, with some transient and partial views of Spithead, and of other parts of the sea, which runs between the Isle of Wight and the coast of Hampshire, but from this commanding seat, a full, extended and complete prospect of the whole length of Spithead, and of every anchored ship therein, and of the towns of Gosport and Portsmouth, burst suddenly and distinctly upon our enraptured sight."

28 Ryde

"Soon after, we were safely and happily landed from our circuitous voyage, at our little port of Ryde, to the inexpressible joy of every part of my company."

Our view has shifted by about 90 degrees, and Regency Ryde spreads itself as if for our inspection. Union Street runs uphill on the right, paralleled by George Street and, closer to us by the small roundabout Dover Street. The mock gothic of Ryde Castle Hotel is to the left, fronting the sea, and here are the recent shoreline developments by Medina Borough Council, now replaced by a Unitary Authority - The Isle of Wight Council - England's first.

Front left is the newly constructed sea wall of Ryde Harbour. To its right the Pavilion, saved only by a sit-in, now fronts the bowling alley and just beyond, on newly reclaimed land, is the Ice Rink, with the Hovercraft Terminal behind. The elegant townscape behind is redolent of the Regency and the early years of Victoria.

Here are the cool lines of Brigstock Terrace, its equally tasteful china collection still stored unseen in Ryde library basement. Past the roundabout is the Prince Consort, once the Royal Victoria Yacht Club, and taking its name from the fact that Prince Albert laid its foundation stone. Up from the pier, itself first constructed in 1813, is Yelf's Hotel of 1810, and Westmacott's Royal Victoria Arcade, opened in 1836, and saved from planned demolition in the early 1970s, after the town council wanted to pull it down. The names of the guilty parties should be engraved on its walls, along with those who saved it.

Gilbert Scott's All Saints dominates the top of the town, its rich and ornate interior denied our view. Behind is enveloping countryside, Haylands Farm - staffed by people with learning difficulties, giving them the chance in life we all deserve - and Upton. Rowlands Wood and Firestone Copse loom to the right; between them lies Havenstreet, our next (inland) port of call. The inland chalk cliff top left betrays the workings at Ashey Down. Out of shot is Ashey sea-mark, and obscured by distance Newport and the Medina, at whose mouth we began, and will end.

"The sea-mark at Ashey is a lofty triangular pyramid of stone; it was erected by Government in the year 1735, and was designedly left unfinished, the apex appearing to have been obliquely cut off. This pyramid is visible from every elevated spot in the Island, and is a direction to the sailor, from almost all the surrounding seas.

The road passes from this pyramid, for nearly three miles, along the ridge of a continuation of Downs, and discloses the country, on each side, in a pleasing variety of interesting points of view, till it enters a lane, which in its regular descent to Newport, shews that town the castle of Carisbrooke, with part of the river from Newport to Cowes, to great advantage."

29 Havenstreet Village

"Black Bridge is thrown across a deep torrent, over which the road passes to Haven Street, consisting of a long line of scattered houses, and probably so denominated from its neighbourhood to the pool of Wootton Bridge."

Havenstreet still spills along the valley floor, like bones of a giant dinosaur with Coppidhall Farm at its head. Blackbridge Brook is a tributary of Wootton Creek and crosses under the road here, feeding the small pool bottom left. At the top of the village Firestone Copse spreads its green tentacles; the small pagoda like building in the steep field looking down on Havenstreet is the War Memorial

Great Wood edges bottom left. Bottom right, Rowlands Lane runs up past Pondcast Farm over the hill to Rowlands Cross, then down past Brickfields riding centre to the outskirts of Binstead, just visible top right. Newnham Farm is middle top, as the land rises to Quarr Hill.

Havenstreet - the words elided together since Wyndham's time - runs down towards us, with an offshoot of the high street bending round in a bow to encompass the Church. To the right is Holmdale, large and slightly sinister, and the community centre: to the left is the White Hart Inn. On the pub wall is preserved an old sign to the railway station, oddly appropriate as we shall see.

The nearest large building to us on the right of the high street is Haven Nursing home, housed in the old hospital building. It has a separate clock tower, and a wooden white painted pagoda on top of the main building - Victorian Gothic in full horror movie mode - which matches the War Memorial at the other end of the village.

The land at the bottom of the picture is scarred with an underground cable trail. A railway track crosses the bottom left hand corner of the picture, still with its track and in working order, though seemingly lost in the middle of nowhere. All will be explained.

30 Havenstreet Railway Station

"The beginning of this morning's ride was through an open and high country, till we came to Combley Lyn, from whence the road chiefly passed to St Helens, for though Combley Wood does not continue beyond Haven-Street, yet other woods are connected with it which are, in general, the property of Sir William Oglander, and whose property is easily ascertained, by the peculiar size and care of its timber."

This remains true. Great Wood in the middle is connected both to Briddlesford Copse and Firestone Copse top left - bisected by Blackbridge Brook - and Moor Wood. The green wedge bottom left is the edge of Combley Great Wood itself, which extends itself almost to Robin Hill Country Park due south.

We have shifted a mile or so south from the previous photo. The bottom of Havenstreet village runs down diagonally towards us. Combley Road runs down under the railway line - leading on the right back to Ryde - and past the triangle of land, itself half wooded, which contains Havenstreet Steam Railway Centre.

Rather like in an episode of the original "Avengers" on ITV, we land in a time warp, a railway station pre-Beeching, with sidings and a marshalling yard. Everything is newly painted, everything is in its right period, even down to the old red telephone box standing outside the Railway Shop and Museum, which itself dates from 1886.

From the car park, a lane leads past a small booking office, and across the railway line to the signal box and station. At the far end is a modern brick cafe, opened in 1982 and built on the Youth Opportunity Programme.   For the young at heart a small adventure playground opens beyond, at the edge of the field. In front, green carriages have been shunted semi-permanently into a siding. At regular intervals, steam trains puff off to the left, and the terminus at Wootton Common, to which we too will now fly.

Unconcerned, cows graze quietly in the fields. Guildford Farm is bottom left, and behind the railway centre, vintage lorries are parked in a corner. They are refugees from history, rock pools which have survived the retreating tide of time, as is the working steam railway, and the dense woodland which invades the picture.

"The immense range of wood, called Combley Wood was part of the possessions of the Abbey of Quarr, which forms one of the most beautiful, finest and compact estates in the kingdom, beginning from the sea, near the abbey ruins, and ending at Hasely Farm, in the parish of Arreton, which includes the space of more than six miles.

Some large fields are intermixed among the brows of this extensive wood, which seem to invite the erection of a mansion-house, and from which nature alone has designed the most magnificent vistas, that expand, through the descending woods, to the valleys below."

31 Wootton

"Upon the point of a hill, called Fernhill, before we descend to Wootton Bridge, is a house built by Mr Orde, the present Governor of the Island. It appears to have been erected upon the plan of a church; a lofty and handsome tower rises from one end, with a large Gothic window near its base, while a single room annexed to the other end, of an inferior height and breadth to the rest of the buiding, denotes the chancel of it."

Wootton is a corruption of "Wood Town", reflecting the Quarr estates from which it was hewn. Even its shape here looks like a giant Christmas tree, its tip surmounted by the Creek. Fernhill is top right, off Packsfield Lane.

The green space in the middle of close packed housing comprises the school playing fields, and a cricket pitch. The road to Newport leads off on the right. Palmers Lane bends back towards us. Parallel but further from the camera is Church Road, and the traffic lights, where Whiterails Road leads off diagonally past Wootton Common - terminus for the steam railway - and down to Staplers. Directly in front of us, Brocks Copse Road leads down past Palmers Farm and Westwood - with its ornate Tudor garden revealed behind the main house - through woodland to Whippingham, our next port of call.

Looking back for the last time, we see Wootton centre, with the Island's only all night supermarket and Minghella's ice cream factory. Beyond the Creek, the road to Quarr leads up Kite Hill and past Fishbourne, with New Copse top left. The Old Mill Pond snakes back towards Havenstreet. Firestone Copse is to the right, half lost in clouds which drift across the picture like smoke, wood's rightful end.

"The Pond, as it is called, though it may at high water well deserve the appellation of a Lake, runs something more than a mile from Wootton Bridge, by a serpentine course, up into the country.

My curiosity induced me to explore the farthest recess of this broad and extensive piece of water, and I hired at the bridge a small flatbottomed boat for the occasion. About half a mile higher, the banks of the water begin to be contracted into a width of about 150 feet, and continue at that breadth, till it receives a brook which rises in Combley wood, and occasionally descends in a rapid torrent, under Black Bridge, near Haven Street.

The whole of this contracted channel wears a solemn gloom, and its winding course quickly conveyed me into a region of the thickest shade, where ancient and decayed oaks exposed their half naked roots from both its banks, while their low and spreading branches impended over and darkened the water beneath them. The gentle acclivities, also, on all sides are covered with coppices and woods, as far as the eye could reach. When the water is expended by the working of the mill, the current exhibits only a sorry brook, meandering through a broad expanse of oozy and offensive mud."

32 Folly Inn, Whippingham

"We rode towards Whippingham, in our way to the Ferry of Cowes. The principal object, from both these roads, is the Newport River, upon which two large Tide Mills project their rival fronts, but there are few coppices to enliven its banks, or to enrich its prospects."

We are looking back from Cowes, due south. The Folly Inn - recycled from the wood of a long wrecked boat - is at the top of the picture, to the east of the Medina as it maintains its stately progress towards Newport Quay. The young Uffa Fox would swim across the river from here, to gather birds eggs. St Mildred's Church, Whippingham, in whose graveyard he now resides, is out of shot top left, behind Kingston Farm. "Enlivening" the west riverbank is Shamblers Copse, with Werrar Farm behind, and - just visible - the curving line of the dismantled Newport to West Cowes railway, now a cycleway.

Recycling is the order of the day hereabouts. "Enriching the prospect" here are the twin towers of Cowes Gas Turbine Station, with cemetery and waste ground in front, leading to the industrial shoreline of East Cowes. The RNLI building is the long shed at the back of the boat park, with Cowes Marina edging out into the river, like white aerials.

33 West Cowes from East Cowes

"We rode to Whippingham Church, from whence we soon recovered the early track of this morning's excursion, which brought us again to Cowes."

This is the previous photograph, turned 90 degrees so that we face across the Medina to West Cowes. The Marina is now bottom left, and Clarence Road leads on to the Floating Bridge past the mysterious sheds of Westland Aerospace.

Across the river, Brittania Wharf and Cowes Sailing Centre and College - gayly striped with yacht designs - front the shore. Far left, the recently constructed Arctic Road Link leads from an industrial estate to Northwood Reservoir and Cemetery - a reservoir of the dead - and bends past a cash and carry supermarket on the old Ronson's site. Light industry yields to wholesale shopping.

In the far distance, Siemans Plessey is top left. Top right, the seashore leads away and off camera, past Egypt Point towards Gurnard and Rew Street. The circle is almost complete.

34 West Cowes

The camera comes in closer, and moves up the West Cowes shore, towards a few hundred yards of where we started. To journey to an Island one needs a boat, and here is FBM Marine, where modern catamarans, patrol craft and monohull ferries are created to cruise the waterways of the world.

Here, where boats have been constructed by family firms for generations, is the new world of international finance. FBM Marine is a British registered company, but itself a subsidiary of the Hong Kong Parkview Group, whose European activities are run from London. Here is the hi-tech world of the future, already here.

Behind, a maze of roads and houses leads to a circular car park, built - I presume - on the site of an old gasometer, almost the end of our journey.

The Isle of Wight is itself an endless circle, round which we could forever travel. It is of manageable size, yet contains a huge variety of landscapes and time zones. One can sail around it in less than a day, drive east to west in at most an hour - depending on the traffic on Coppins Bridge - or walk around it at one's leisure in a week. I hope that this book, which can be flicked through in a few minutes, is something the reader will return to over the years.

I am told that the view from the top of the radio mast at Chillerton provides the best terrestial viewpoint of the whole Island, though was not informed precisely how one reached such private and dizzy heights. There are easier vantage points. Five Barrows Down above Brighstone, the summit of Carisbrooke Castle, the sea mark of Ashey Down on a clear day: all give close to a bird's eye - or aerial - view to the keen walker. Wyndham attempted an overview from the last of these prominences.

"The harbour of Brading, the peninsular of Bimbridge, the rich woods around Nunwell and their continuation to Wootton Bridge are all overlooked on the east and the north side, while the broad and fertile vale of Newchurch, extending to the mountainous hills of Shanklin and St Catherine's, the steep precipices of which, on their opposite sides, bound what is called the Undercliff, court the eye to the southward.

A more extensive view opens to the westward, which passes over the dreary heath of Parkhurst Forest, and is lost on the naked downs of Brixton, Afton and the Freshwater Cliffs."

The Island can shrink, in turn, to an ordnance survey map, folded in a back pocket, or to a child's paddling pool at Ventnor, to be stepped over. It can also encompass forever. Our final photograph typifies Island history, an ancient landscape surmounted by a spectacular and man-made structure, of venerable antiquity. But on the Isle of Wight, as we have so often found, all is not as it seems ...